SECRET
SOCIETIES

CONGRÈS RÉGIONAL DES LOGES D'ÎLE DE FRANCE

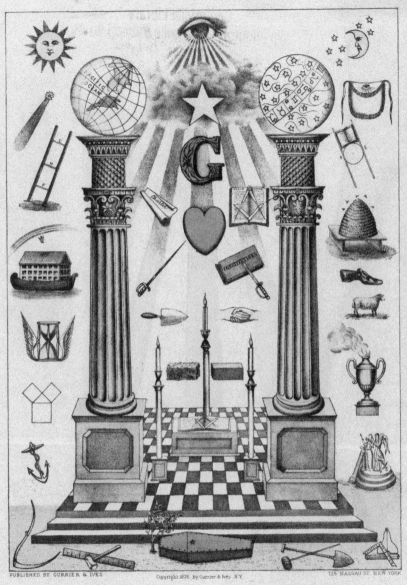

PUBLISHED BY CURRIER & IVES

115 NASSAU ST. NEW YORK

THE MASONIC CHART.

SECRET
SOCIETIES

UNMASKING THE
ILLUMINATI, FREEMASONS,
AND KNIGHTS TEMPLAR

LIGHTNING
GUIDES

ISBN Print 978-1-942411-50-5
eBook 978-1-942411-51-2

> **"We are as a people inherently and historically opposed to secret societies, to secret oaths, and to secret proceedings."**
>
> **—JOHN F. KENNEDY**

We live in a world where the marks of secret societies are all around us—some of them hidden in plain view, others masked in centuries of myth and legend. George Washington was a Freemason, and performed Masonic rites at the laying of the cornerstone of the US Capital. Mozart, too, was a Mason and satirized Masonic initiation rituals in his opera *The Magic Flute*. Presidents from George Bush to Benjamin Franklin have been members of secret societies. As have powerful families, titans of industry, politicians and intellectuals across nations and centuries. Do these shadowy organizations exist to control and influence the path of human affairs? Do they watch over us, or prey upon us? Who are their members, how are they chosen, and what powers do they wield? If only we could speak to the initiated, what illumination might we find?

CONTENTS

INTRODUCTION

D o you want to know a secret? Every time you close a door, you invite questions. Sometimes these questions are so small or mundane, they barely register as thoughts. But in other instances, a closed door can trigger a desire to know more, a burning curiosity that gets people speculating about what's happening on the other side.

That's why secret societies have always been so fascinating. When a group of people closes the door to the outside world, we have to wonder what's going on. Sometimes important things are afoot—like the Freemason meetings of the turn of the 18th century, when George Washington, James Monroe, and Andrew Jackson were members. Other times, not so much. Just because a meeting of your local garden committee is closed to the public, it doesn't mean they're plotting world domination … right?

Secret societies come in all shapes and sizes. Some are religious. Some are political. Some are focused on achieving a specific goal. Some have completely anonymous memberships, and some are so secretive that we can't even be sure they really exist. Talking about secret societies poses a conundrum: We don't know enough about them to separate the facts from the endless rumors and suspicions. Most of the time, all we can do is press our ear to the door.

Whether they're secretly pulling the strings of the entire world order, or simply making us think twice about those shady people on the local garden committee, secret societies have a very real effect on our daily lives. Maybe, if we stare at the puzzle long enough, we'll begin to put the pieces together.

NEW MEMBERS OF THE
SKULL AND BONES
ARE GIVEN A GRANDFATHER CLOCK
AND $15,000 CASH

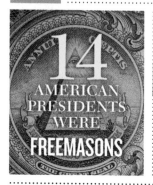

14 AMERICAN PRESIDENTS WERE FREEMASONS

"ASSASSIN"
FROM ARABIC *HAŠĪŠĪ*, MEANING
"HASHISH USER":
MEDIEVAL MUSLIM SECT
REPUTED TO USE HASHISH
BEFORE GOING ON FANATICAL
MURDER SPREES

JOHN F. KENNEDY
WAS A MEMBER OF THE IRISH FRATERNAL ORGANIZATION
THE ANCIENT ORDER
of **HIBERNIANS**

MEMBERS OF CONGREGATION FOR THE LIGHT
BELIEVE THAT THROUGH "PROPER LIVING"
THEY WILL BE SPARED THE DESTRUCTION OF EARTH AND
MOVE TO A PLANET CALLED NAY

What is a secret society?

Secret societies are clubs or organizations whose beliefs, motives, teachings, and practices are hidden from non-members. Depending on the society, members either elect to join or are selected by the society from the populace. Members can also be born into the society, although this is rare.

Why do secret societies form?

The reasons secret societies form are as varied as the societies themselves. For instance, the Thule Society of early-20th-century Germany gathered to "preserve the Aryan race." It sponsored the German Workers' Party, a predecessor of the Nazi Party. Not all secret societies are destructive, however. Some have formed to subvert cruel governmental regimes, advocate for the underprivileged, or free enslaved communities.

Are secret societies legal?

In the United States it is perfectly legal to form and belong to a secret society. They are protected under the First Amendment of the US Constitution. However, group and individual actions taken by secret societies may be illegal, depending on the nature of the actions. For example, Ku Klux Klan members are frequently in the news for committing hate crimes, but it is not illegal to gather, make hateful speeches, or publish hate-mongering literature.

What was the first secret society?

Anthropologists trace the earliest secret societies to the all-male Germanic *männerbund*, or "blood brothers." The männerbund worshipped the war god Odin, and learned secret esoteric teachings from elders. The larger archaic German society held männerbund societies in higher regard than the family unit. Bonds between blood brothers were so powerful that they were believed to extend into the afterlife.

Can a religion be considered a secret society?

Some religions have exclusive subsects whose motives and practices are highly secretive. The Druze, for instance, is an Islamic group known to disguise its beliefs and blend into the larger community. Even internally, the group reserves the most sacred teachings for members who demonstrate the greatest intellect and insight.

Who are the Freemasons?

The Freemasons are a worldwide secret society officially dating back to June 24, 1717, with the founding of the Grand Lodge of England. The Freemasons claim to be a secular society, but its requirement that members believe in an omnipresent Supreme Being has led skeptics to call this claim into question. To become a member, one must be inducted through a series of initiations involving lectures and reenactments of the construction of the Temple of Solomon. There is no central authority in Freemasonry. Instead, Masonic lodges are self-governed by region.

THE MOST FEUDAL SYSTEM

WHAT WAS IT ABOUT FEUDALISM THAT GAVE RISE TO SOME OF THE MOST WELL-KNOWN SOCIETIES?

The Middle Ages (500 to 1500), one of darkest periods in human history, were marked by difficulty and calamity. From the fall of the Roman Empire to the beginning of the European Renaissance, these thousand years of brutality and bloodshed were a terrifying time to exist. The dissolution of the Roman Empire resulted in a paroxysm of regional conflicts from Anatolia (modern-day Turkey) to Spain in the east and west, and from England to Egypt in the north and south. Merciless battles between Christians and pagans, Vikings, and Muslims often spared no one. With people jostling for food, land, and power,

Right: The early-12th-century seat of the Order of the Assassins.

two secret warrior societies arose to protect their own interests. How did the monarchical political systems of their respective times influence their power and reach?

ALL CLUES LEAD TO ROME

Charles the Great (742–814), also known as Charlemagne, the first king of the Holy Roman Empire, led a fierce campaign to convert all of Europe to Roman Catholicism. He divided the continent into 350 counties, with a count presiding over each. These counts assisted in a massive campaign to improve children's education with programs naturally designed to indoctrinate youth with church teachings, and all counts reported to the king. Charles the Great had little tolerance for pagans and other non-Catholics. He drew the line quite clearly in the Massacre of Verden, where he ordered 4,500 Saxons murdered in Lower Saxony for practicing the Germanic paganism of their ancestors.

As Charles the Great and his successors worked on fortifying Europe with a strong Roman Catholic identity, Islam was working its way through the former territory of the Roman Empire. Although it was a relatively new religion, Islam spread rapidly. Before the Prophet Muhammad died in AD 632, he united the Arabian Peninsula in a single Arab polity. Only decades after Muhammad's passing, Umar ibn al-Khattab, the third caliph of Islam, led a military campaign that swept the Sassanid Persian Empire and brought two-thirds of the Eastern Roman Empire under Islamic rule. Included in the siege was the Holy Land, the area between the Jordan River and the Mediterranean Sea. The caliphate was proud to preside over Jerusalem, but it would lose the land in the First Crusade at the turn of the millennium.

THE FIRST CRUSADE

The First Crusade (1096–1099) began with an appeal to Pope Urban II by the Byzantine Emperor Alexios I Komnenos, who asked for volunteers to assist him in repelling the Seljuq Turks from Anatolia. In his appeal to the pope, Komnenos made an ancillary request for help taking Jerusalem back from the Muslims. Pope Urban II agreed to assist Komnenos and, in a rousing sermon given to church leaders at the Council of Clermont in France, sent a call to the European monarchs to gather troops for war. The resulting army was a fierce group of knights, peasants, and serfs from France, England, the Holy Roman Empire, Normandy, Flanders, and other nations. Led by vanguard military leaders, the first crusaders trekked to Constantinople, where they strategized their next move. Along the way, Komnenos's request for help recapturing of the Holy Land became the primary goal of the crusaders, whose hearts were then set on Christian hegemony in Jerusalem.

[
1935 The year Nazi architect Wilhelm Hübotter designed the Saxon Grove, a memorial for those who were killed at the Massacre of Verden.
]

DID YOU KNOW

To motivate Christians to reclaim the Holy Land from Muslims, Pope Urban II promised forgiveness of all sins to anyone that participated in the Crusades. Even soldiers who engaged in the worst types of sin—rape, murder, robbery—were thought to go to heaven if they fought in the Crusades.

MASONIC KNIGHTS

The Masonic Order of the Knights Templar takes new members by invitation only. These members must already be high-ranking royal arch Masons or master Masons.

THE ASSASSINS: A SOCIETY OF KILLERS

In 1099 the crusaders launched a merciless assault on the Muslim and Jewish occupants of Jerusalem, decimating them. Over the next few months, a motley grouping of Bulgarians, Syrians, Greeks, and Christians from other nations repopulated Jerusalem. Little did they know that a vigilante opposition group known as the Assassins was patrolling the area. The Assassins were founded by Hassan-i Sabbah, an Ismaili religious fanatic, in the late 1080s. Hassan was a zealous proselytizer who, after years of praising the merits of Ismailism, had amassed many followers. Upon finding headquarters in the mountain castle of Alamut (in modern-day Iran), Hassan inducted men into his secret society of killers, whose mission was to spread Ismailism and strike down opposition, including the Seljuqs and the newly arrived Christians.

> **1139** Pope Innocent II issues a papal bull (or charter) called "Every Perfect Gift," officially approving of the Knights Templar. This bull made the Knights a sovereign papal entity, granting them immunity throughout Western Christendom.

Because of the Mongol invasion of the Alamut castle in 1256, little is known about the inner workings of the Assassins. Alamut Castle was embedded in a mountaintop, only accessible via a heavily patrolled, narrow dirt path. The order was a five-tiered hierarchal system, with Hassan and his successors as the grand master, followed by the great propagandists, propagandists, companions, and adherents. The adherents were the front-line fighters of the Assassins, and Hassan is said to have indoctrinated them to kill for Ismailism by getting them high on hashish while he delivered bombastic speeches.

Adherents of the Assassin society were told they would reach paradise for killing opposition leaders, and they were trained to do so by first befriending those leaders. Hassan taught his followers the languages and cultures of their victims, preparing followers to get close to top-ranking opposition officials.

SECRET ROAD PATROL: THE KNIGHTS TEMPLAR

A similarly subversive secret warrior society, called the Knights Templar, cropped up in the decades after Hassan founded the Assassins. The Knights Templar adamantly protected Christian interests.

The Knights Templar began with the vision of a French nobleman named Hugues de Payens. Having ventured to the Holy Land with Count Hugh de Champagne, Payens encountered dangers along the route to Jerusalem. The roads were rife with thieves and murderers, and pilgrims taking the route were never sure they would make it to the Holy Land alive. Payens took action on behalf of the pilgrims, gathering eight of his knight relatives and forming an order of knights to protect the roads.

Portrait of James of Mola, Grand Master of the Knights Templar, from *Le Livre Rouge—Histoire de l'Échafaud en France* by Dupray de La Maherie, 1863.

Like other monastic orders, these knights took vows of poverty and chastity.

Shortly after founding the order in 1118, Payens approached King Baldwin II of Jerusalem to discuss the order's purpose. Baldwin found Payens's intentions noble and granted his order use of the Templum Solomonis (modern-day Al-Asqa Mosque) for its headquarters. As the order grew in size and popularity, it became known as the Poor Fellow-Soldiers of Christ and of the Temple of Solomon, a name that was shortened to Knights Templar. In battle, they wore a distinctive paramilitary uniform consisting of a white mantle and a red cross. Harsh initiation rites were enforced on new members to test their willpower for the road ahead.

The Knights Templar proved to be an imposing force during the Crusades. They never retreated in battle, and they defeated armies many times their size through ingenious tactical skills. One key victory that demonstrated their strength was at the Battle of Montgisard in 1177. Using a combination of wit and brawn, a mere 80 Knights Templar confronted a Muslim army of 26,000 soldiers. The Muslim army's leader, Saladin, had met the small entourage in Gaza. He foolishly laughed at the number of the Knights Templar and headed south for Egypt. The Templars remained in Gaza, where they joined King Baldwin's forces. Together they trailed Saladin south and pinned his army in a nighttime ambush in Montgisard. By morning, only a tenth of the Muslim army had survived, and the Knights Templar were hailed as heroes throughout Western Christendom.

The Templars evolved into a society of warrior-bankers, and over time their money and influence enabled them to build forts across continental Europe and on the outskirts of Jerusalem. However, when the Crusades ended and the dream of conquering Jerusalem faded, the Knights Templar fell out of favor. Eventually they were driven from existence by the very church that had chartered them in the first place. Nevertheless, the legacy of the Knights Templar remains, and Masonic scholars consider them the forerunners of Freemasonry.

FEAR THE GAVEL: THE GERMAN VEHMGERICHT

At the dawn of the Middle Ages, the region we know today as Germany was in chaos. Bands of outlaws roamed the forests, and mercenaries fought warriors in illegal street battles. Travel was safe for no one, and safety measures were urgently needed. Into this power vacuum came the German Vehmgericht, a fraternal organization of judges under the jurisdiction of the Holy Roman Empire. It held secret courts in Westphalia to try, sentence, and execute criminals. Lay judges decided cases presided over by a chairman. Beneath the judges were Freifronen, the lowest-ranking initiates, who were assigned to maintain order and carry out executions. Any German man of "pure blood" could be initiated, and many nobles became judges, including the Italian Emperor Sigismund, who would become the Holy Roman Emperor in 1431. Members at all three tiers of the Vehmgericht were taught secret hand signals, allowing them to recognize one another, and given knives engraved with the letters SSGG. Nobody outside the courts knew what the letters stood for, but the knives were left next to the bodies of the dead to broadcast that the execution was the handiwork of the Vehmgericht.

The overarching power of the Vehmgericht corrupted its members, who became known for unjustly sentencing men to death as a form of personal vendetta. By the end of the 16th century the Holy Roman Emperor Maximilian realized that the group had become unruly, and members of the Vehmgericht were relegated to municipal police duties. In 1811, the king of Westphalia dismantled them altogether. The Vehmgericht re-emerged briefly at the beginning of the Nazi era, but its members were later crushed by the Nazi Party.

Right: The burning of Templars (From: *De Casibus Virorum Illustrium* by Giovanni Boccaccio). Found in the collection of the British Library.

SMOKE &
MIRRORS

SECRET SOCIETIES
OF THE SILVER SCREEN

Secret societies and hidden artifacts have long been fodder for Hollywood scripts. In the film *National Treasure* (2004), historian and cryptologist Benjamin Gates (Nicolas Cage) searches for a treasure once protected by the Knights Templar and later hidden by the Freemasons during the American Revolution. Hidden treasure is also the theme of *Indiana Jones: The Last Crusade* (1989), where archaeologist Indiana Jones (Harrison Ford) searches for the Holy Grail in a race against the Nazis. *The Matrix* (1999) is one of the most-referenced films featuring secret societies and subversion. In this iconic film, Neo (Keanu Reeves) is invited by Morpheus (Laurence Fishburne) to join a tiny society of "real" humans. The society lives aboard the *Nebuchadnezzar* ship, isolated from a world lost to the tyranny of fully conscious machines.

The movie world is filled with Illuminati symbolism. The society has been mentioned in *Lara Croft: Tomb Raider* (2001), in which a group calling itself the Illuminati plots to take over the world. The group claims it can fulfill a 4,000-year-old dream of world hegemony.

FROM TEMPLES TO LODGES

MASONIC ARCHITECTURE AND IDENTITY IN SECRET SOCIETIES

To a Freemason, a lodge is both a physical place and a term for the members, who consider themselves lodge brothers. Each Masonic lodge is named by its founding member or members. When a town or city includes multiple lodges, lodge names contain a number (for example, Bronx Lodge No. 29). Numbers are registered with the governing council, allowing all the lodges in a local jurisdiction to maintain control and a level of secrecy.

{ **Masonic Lodge** (noun): 1. The congregation of people who gather at Freemason meetings. 2. The buildings Freemasons meet in. }

Lodge rooms are modeled after spaces in the Temple of King Solomon. In the Middle Ages, stonemasons who learned their building trade in guilds modeled large construction projects on biblical descriptions. As they became less involved as builders, they formed a more philosophical organization. Part of their symbolism and pageantry dates to the symbolism in Solomon's temple. To the Freemasons, the Temple of King Solomon is the pinnacle of architectural achievement. The temple inspired classical Greek architecture, including Corinthian, Ionic, and Doric columns. Legend has it that the roots of geometry were founded on two pillars of the temple, and the principles of geometry, needed by skilled Masons in their building trade, were passed down from the gods to the masons. Later, the Freemasons were influenced by Renaissance architecture, elevating the architect to an exalted place in Renaissance society.

Masonic lodges fall into one of three designations—blue, craft, and ancient—each referring to lodges of the first three Masonic degrees. The term "craft lodge" is mostly used in England. The blue lodge refers to the traditional colors of the Irish or English Freemasons. The term "mother lodge" identifies the actual place where a lodge member passed initiation and earned his apprentice degree. A daughter lodge is usually under a larger, local jurisdiction.

THE HALL OF SKULL AND BONES

The Hall of Skull and Bones is on the grounds of Yale University, in New Haven, Connecticut. Also known as the Tomb, it was built in three phases. Wing one was completed in 1856, wing two in 1903, and the towers in 1912. Most of it features a neo-Gothic style. Its original architect's identity is uncertain, but most historians have narrowed possibilities down to Alexander Davis and Henry Austin. The last addition to the Tomb was a wrought-iron fence surrounding the main building. The Skull and Bones society also owns and manages a retreat on Deer Island in the St. Lawrence River, secluded enough for its members to hold private meetings and retreats. It has fallen into disrepair in recent years, but members still visit, affectionately calling the place a dump.

THE BOHEMIAN GROVE

Each summer some of the world's richest and most influential men meet for two weeks of summer camp at the Bohemian Grove, an almost 3,000-acre compound in Monte Rio, California. The exclusive men's club has hosted Richard Nixon, Ronald Reagan, George H. W. Bush, and countless other influential figures. Though no woman has ever been given full membership, there have been a few honorary female members in the organization's history, but they are not invited to participate in the summer meeting.

The club's mascot is an owl, which symbolizes wisdom and knowledge. The Bohemian Club's patron saint is John of Nepomuk. According to the club's folklore, he suffered at the hands of a Bohemian monarch because he did not disclose the secrets of the queen. A wood-carved statue of St. John greets visitors to the grove. The statue depicts St. John with a finger over his lips, reminding all to keep the activities at the grove a secret.

(INTER)NATIONAL TREASURE

RELIC HUNTERS HAVE
SEARCHED FOR CENTURIES,
BUT DO SECRET SOCIETIES
HOLD ANCIENT TREASURES?

One of the many fascinating aspects of secret societies is the idea that they have somehow smuggled ancient relics throughout the ages. These items—equal parts history and hearsay—supposedly offer magical powers, eternal life, or a closer connection with the divine. But is there any evidence that these treasures reside within the meeting halls of clandestine organizations?

THE HOLY GRAIL

The Holy Grail first appeared in Chrétien de Troyes's half-written romance poem, *Perceval le Conte du Graal*, as a processional salver. Other writers, attempting to finish his work, made a legend out of the Holy Grail. Over time it became synonymous with all things unobtainable. In later Christian literature, the Holy Grail is the cup Jesus used to serve wine at the Last Supper. At Christ's crucifixion, the cup was supposed to have received the blood of Christ as it

The Ark of the Covenant on wheels. Stone carving from the Capernaum synagogue, circa 4th century AD.

flowed from his body. It mysteriously disappeared from the scene, but according to folklore it was brought to England by Joseph of Arimathea, after which its location was kept secret.

The knights of King Arthur's court were determined to find the holy cup. They searched a castle surrounded by moats and guarded by the Fisher King. Some myths built around the Holy Grail contend that it had magic healing properties. King Arthur stood to gain eternal recognition if his knights could find the Holy Grail. To his dismay, they never did.

In literature, the Holy Grail appears in the works of Alfred Lord Tennyson and Sir Walter Scott. In art, it is pictured in the works of Italian painter Simone Martini as a spice pot, Bernardino Luini as a perfume jar, and Frederick Sandys as an ointment cup. German composer Richard Wagner dedicated his last opera, *Parsifal*, to the Holy Grail, adapting the story from the medieval poem of the same name written by Wolfram von Eschenbach.

THE SHROUD OF TURIN

Historians debate whether the Shroud of Turin encased the crucified body of Jesus. Some dismiss the connection as a hoax perpetuated by an artist or someone who wanted to create a legacy by making the claim. Either way, the shroud is one of the most scrutinized and studied garments in history. With the advent of the X-ray machine at the turn of the 20th century, many people thought that the mystery could be scientifically solved. Yet the studies continue and the mystery has deepened.

Some of the substantiating evidence that the Shroud of Turin was indeed the burial cloth of Jesus is that the tears on the cloth correspond to the wounds inflicted on Jesus's body, with the wounds' shape and size similar to those caused by the lances that stabbed him. The body that lay beneath this shroud was buried like others who suffered violent deaths at the time. His body would not have been washed, explaining the stains on the burial garment.

There was no definitive record of the shroud until its first historical mention in the early 14th century. Bishop Pierre d'Arcis wrote a letter to Pope Clement VII stating that the shroud was a forgery and that no attention should be paid

THE STORIED ARK

New scholarship supports a theory that the Ark of the Covenant was taken from Jerusalem during the reign of King Solomon. According to this theory, the descendants of Menelik—today's black Jews of Ethiopia—hold onto it for safekeeping.

to it. It arrived in Turin, Italy, in 1578 and has been on display only a few times, mainly because of security concerns. Four hundred years later, in 1978, the shroud was displayed in Turin and attracted more than 3.5 million spectators. The next public viewing is scheduled for 2025.

THE ARK OF THE COVENANT

One of the great biblical mysteries is the location of the Ark of the Covenant. Thrust into the public consciousness by the hit movie *Raiders of the Lost Ark,* the Ark of the Covenant has been the subject of intensive searches. Mount Nebo, on the east bank of the Jordan River, has been suggested as one possibility. Other possible locations include the west bank of the river, or the Dead Sea. The site is assumed to be near the site of the discovery of the Dead Sea Scrolls, in the caves of Qumran.

The Ark of the Covenant is a storage chest that allegedly contained the tablets of the Ten Commandments as well as Aaron's rod, a jar of manna, and the first Torah scroll. The Ark is an essential artifact of Jewish history and Christian tradition. It remains a source of mystery and a controversial subject in religious scholarship and popular culture.

The Israeli government has welcomed archaeologists searching for the Ark in tunnels beneath the streets of Jerusalem. Researchers speculate that the Ark may lie near the crucifixion site of Jesus, also known as Gordon's Calvary. Some ultra-Orthodox Jewish scholars at the Temple Institute in Old Jerusalem say that the Ark is under the Temple Mount and promise that it will be revealed when the temple is rebuilt.

WHO'S WHO?

A LOOK INSIDE THE MOST STORIED AND FASCINATING SECRET SOCIETIES

Though "secret societies" is a slight misnomer given the amount of information we have about certain groups, their intricate workings are shrouded in a layer of mystery. The Freemasons, Knights Templar, and and other groups have such extensive histories that some secrets have leaked into public awareness.

FREEMASONS

Freemasonry is a fraternal organization comprising members who meet for friendship, brotherhood, charitable work, and personal growth. Freemasonry originated in early 18th century Europe when stonemason guilds formed the first Grand Lodge in England. Unity among skilled tradesmen was appealing. For

A WOMAN IN THE RANKS

Madame de Xaintrailles is one woman who did join a Masonic lodge. Xaintrailles had disguised herself as a man to join the French army and later became a high-ranking officer. Because of her military accomplishments, Xaintrailles was admitted to the Lodge of Frères-Artistes, completely undisguised.

the first time in centuries, men gathered to discuss the ideals of religious freedom, equality, public school education, and democracy. It was not long before lodges were built in cities and towns throughout Europe and the American colonies. Some of the earliest Freemasons were John Hancock, Paul Revere, and Chief Justice John Marshall. These late-18th-century Masons fought proudly in the American Revolution and were major proponents of the Bill of Rights. Debates about the Bill of Rights took place in Masonic lodges.

In a time before social welfare was made available through government programs, Masonic lodges acted as safety nets for the lower classes. Masons founded homes for orphans, widows, and the elderly, and they sponsored meals for the hungry, a tradition that continues. The Freemasons spend an estimated $1.5 million annually in charity. Altruism of this magnitude reflects not only the far reaches of Freemasonry (there are lodges worldwide, including Antarctica Lodge No. 777), but also its basic tenets: brotherly love, truth, and relief. While these tenets appear secular, Freemasons believe that these ideals are predicated on belief in a supreme god. Therefore, they do not admit atheists, a policy that casts doubt on the group's claim that it is secular.

Postcard of Skull and Bones Society Building.

Freemasonry's practices are steeped in tradition, from the floor plan and seating arrangements of their lodges to their garments and member-ranking system. A rectangular floor plan forms the base of every lodge, with cardinal points indicating the seating arrangement of the various ranks. The highest-ranking Mason is the worshipful master, who sits in the east with the treasurer to his right and secretary to his left. Beneath him in rank are the senior and junior wardens, who act as master when necessary. The senior warden sits opposite the master on the west side, and the junior warden sits in the middle of the south side. Next in line are the deacons (two in every lodge—one senior and one junior), who carry messages from the master to the wardens. The senior deacon sits in front of the master, to his right. The junior deacon sits to the right of the senior warden.

Stewards are beneath deacons in rank and fulfill assistant roles as understudies for deacons, usually handling catering and wine service at lodge meals. Stewards sit in the north and south sections, where two rows of seating line the walls. Finally, below the steward is the tyler, who guards the outside of the lodge with a drawn sword, protecting meetings from nonmembers and providing maintenance to lodge rooms.

Mason membership requirements are fairly basic, keeping Freemasonry accessible to new members. Aside from an age minimum (determined by the state the lodge is in), members must have a good reputation in the community and a willingness to uphold the tenets. A member of a Masonic lodge wears a lambskin apron (reminiscent of the aprons the early stonemasons wore to store their tools), pins, and lapels with Masonic emblems (such as the square and compass, also a nod to the original stonemasons). Higher-ranking members are naturally more decorated than stewards and tylers.

Upon joining a lodge, members receive a Masonic Bible, which is a New Testament with a special index of passages quoted in lodge rituals.

Masons are privy to the secrets of the society that make Freemasonry so mysterious to outsiders. Members learn identifying handshakes and passwords. Over time they learn secrets designed to produce inner changes within the individual Mason.

SKULL AND BONES

Probably the most well-known collegiate secret society in America is the Skull and Bones, founded at Yale University in 1832 by Alphonso Taft, the father of future President William Howard Taft. Skull and Bones has come to signify everything that the public sometimes finds both attractive and repulsive about "the elite." To qualify for membership, one must be a

FRATERNITIES

Freemasonry is a fraternal organization that differs from college fraternities in that it's not associated with universities. College fraternities require that members are students of the school, and they are usually given Greek letter names (such as "Phi Beta Kappa," the first college fraternity in the United States). Similar to Masonic lodges, they are self-governed, but there is nothing in the college fraternity system analogous to the Grand Lodge. Masonic lodges are also uniform in regard to who they allow as members, whereas college fraternities make distinctions. For instance, some college fraternities are exclusive by academic major. College fraternities, especially those at the undergraduate level, tend to have hazing initiations that humble and humiliate the initiate over the course of weeks.

male junior-class member at Yale and come from an influential family, preferably one of financial means. Potential members are "tapped," a secret and exclusive solicitation for membership that only occurs once a year, on Tap Day. Outsiders refer to members as Bonesmen.

Upon successful initiation, each new member is given $15,000 and a grandfather clock. Unlike the stereotype of other college fraternities, Skull and Bones is not a typical funhouse with keg parties. Instead it concerns itself with the success of members in the years after graduation. Skull and Bones alumni constitute some of the most famous names in America, among them Goodyear, Pillsbury, Kellogg, and Vanderbilt. While it is a more serious

> **John F. Kerry** was "tapped" to become a Bonesman after spending time abroad with his diplomat father. Around the time of his initiation, he crossed paths with the man he would come to challenge for the presidency in 2004, George W. Bush.

collegiate organization, which began taking female members in 1990, Skull and Bones does engage in one sophomoric antic called "crooking," in which members steal keepsakes from other societies at Yale.

Speculation has grown about the actual activities of Skull and Bones. Its headquarters, referred to forebodingly as "the Tomb," along with rumors that the skulls of Geronimo, Martin Van Buren, and Pancho Villa are hidden within, leave outsiders to imagine the most macabre of rituals. Conspiracy theorists believe Skull and Bones controls the Central Intelligence Agency and that it is a branch of the infamous Illuminati. Writer and researcher Antony C. Sutton wrote one of the most extensive volumes on the Skull and Bones society, *America's Secret Establishment: An Introduction to the Order of Skull & Bones* (1986). Sutton's work provides compelling evidence that Skull and Bones has unprecedented influence on world business, governments, and militaries.

ILLUMINATI

The Illuminati is a secret society of powerful people known for their deep influence on the media, religion, medicine, finance, and government. The Illuminati is feared for its malevolent aims and alleged conspiracy to implement a New World Order, designed to unite the world under a single totalitarian government. Conspiracy theorists detect Illuminati signs and symbols

UNIONS

Though today's labor unions are far from secret, they do share common origins with groups like the Freemasons—membership based on a skilled trade. Unions' guiding belief is that unity is a progressive force against exploitative employers. Unions meet to discuss pay raises and benefits, but unlike the Freemasons (who wear uniforms), union meetings do not require uniforms and do not stage reenactments. Labor unions are categorized by the trade of the laborer. There are unions for painting, teaching, bus driving, and countless other professions. Freemasons do not divide themselves in this fashion, and there is nothing in trade unions that is analogous to Freemasonry's hierarchical structure. The most significant difference is that unions advocate for workers' daily lives, whereas societies such as the Freemasons focus on recreation and charity.

---

on currency, in music videos and songs, and even on news stations. The theorists connect natural disasters and terrorist attacks with the Illuminati, alleging that the group aims to manipulate our emotions and energy as fuel for its projects. But without an official emblem or headquarters, the Illuminati resist conclusive identification as a society of individuals and are sometimes perceived as simply the product of a paranoid imagination.

On May 1, 1776, Adam Weishaupt, a Bavarian professor of canon law at the University of Ingolstadt, along with four students, founded a secret society called the Bavarian Illuminati. Weishaupt and the students were tired of the university's promotion of

Jesuit beliefs in the classroom. They believed in the power of the individual and the ideal that true education is free of political and religious influence. Together, these men spread the ideals of the Enlightenment, including religious freedom and democracy.

Fearing the rise of insurgent groups, the Bavarian ruler Charles Theodore outlawed all secret societies in Bavaria, including the Illuminati and the Freemasons. With support from the Roman Catholic Church, these societies were banned in the mid-1780s. However, even with only a few years in operation, the Bavarian Illuminati formed a fairly sophisticated society. New members were "novices," midlevel members were "Minerval," and high-ranking members the "Illuminated Minerval." Membership was exclusive to male Christians between 18 to 30, with women, Jews, and pagans explicitly banned. Weishaupt looked at the character of potential members before granting them novice status. He preferred a pliant mind and docile nature, and he looked down on empty pockets, favoring wealthy young men above all.

The Illuminati's most important goal was establishing a new paradigm for people to live free of imperial tyranny. Weishaupt saw the Roman Catholic Church and the Bavarian crown as evil entities colluding to subjugate the masses. By contrast, a governing system employing his ideals would be intellectually superior and promote religious freedom. Weishaupt published his beliefs in exile in *A Complete History of the Persecutions of the Illuminati in*

Nesta Helen Webster is largely credited with reviving the theory of the Illuminati. In 1920, Webster wrote a series of anti-Semitic articles for London's *Morning Post*, stating that the Illuminati is controlled by Jews, Jesuits, and Freemasons. She accused the Illuminati of causing World War I and the Bolshevik Revolution.

18th-century French allegorical Masonic seals.

Bavaria (1785). Later, *Proofs of a Conspiracy* (1798), by John Robinson, claimed the Illuminati had been the biggest threat to society and that Bavaria would do well to rid itself of the group. However, within Robinson's work were suggestions that the Illuminati was still alive and that it was planning world domination. Robinson's book, along with *Memoirs Illustrating the History of Jacobinism* (1798), by Augustin Barruel, promoted a theory that the Illuminati had caused the French Revolution and would conduct subversions throughout the world. Robinson's and Barruel's books were so compelling that they were cited in church sermons on the other side of the Atlantic. These sermons were also printed in New England newspapers to warn the public against the Illuminati, whatever it was, whoever they were.

Some of today's most influential people are alleged to belong to the Illuminati—from Angelina Jolie and Beyoncé to British

Prime Minister James Cameron, German Chancellor Angela Merkel, and former President George H. W. Bush. As the theories go, high-profile members "give away" their Illuminati status by flashing the "Roc," or pyramid sign, with their hands. This pyramid appears on the back of the US one-dollar bill, the design of which has been in circulation since 1935. Beneath the pyramid is the Latin inscription "Novus Ordo Seclorum," which can be loosely translated as "New World Order." Theorists also claim that the Illuminati's media control manipulates our minds, making us docile and vulnerable to coded messages and corruption. Because television, radio, and digital media come our way through limited frequency bands, these media are considered perfect tools of persuasion.

THE ROSICRUCIANS

The origin of the Rosicrucian society is nebulous. In 1614, a pamphlet titled *Fame of the Brotherhood of the RC* was published in Cassel, Germany, by an unknown author. The pamphlet tells the tale of a man named Christian Rosenkreuz who lived 120 years earlier. Rosenkreuz allegedly walked the Near East, learning the secrets of the universe from gifted Arabian and Egyptian mystics. Inspired to teach others, he returned to Germany and formed the Rosicrucians, a society of eight men to whom he divulged his esoteric teachings. According to *Fame of the Brotherhood*, the Rosicrucians functioned in secret for 100 years, but by 1614 the public was deemed ready to learn about the society's teachings. The German public found the pamphlet fascinating, and two more books were mysteriously published: *The Confession of the Brotherhood RC* (1615) and *The Chemical*

CULTS

Cults differ significantly from groups like the Freemasons, mainly due to cults' religious underpinnings. The word "cult" carries negative undertones of brainwashing, doomsday prophecy, and a subversive power dynamic between cult leaders and members. Like the Freemasons, cults have rituals, but their main emphasis is on religious belief. The Freemasons emphasize ritual and deemphasize religious belief. Cults typically have long-term aims; this is especially the case with doomsday prophecy cults, in which members prepare themselves for the end of time. Masonic lodges, by contrast, are more life-affirming. They promote the Masons of the order and engage with the outside world for charity. Cults tend to withdraw from the world for fear of outside influence, and if they raise money, it is almost always for themselves.

Wedding of Christian Rosenkreuz (1616). In *Confession*, we are told of a new age to come, when society will be reformed to a state of grace. *Chemical Wedding* describes a form of alchemy within the body, whereby one transcends into spiritual gold through personal enlightenment.

Within the pamphlets were the rules of the Rosicrucian order:

- Members can only use their knowledge to heal, and they must never do so in exchange for payment.
- All members must attend the annual meeting at the Spiritus Sanctus.
- Before dying, every member must look for a successor.
- The organization must be kept a secret for 100 years.

Rosicrucian cross in a cemetery in Roslin, Scotland.

The folklore of the Rosicrucians was romanticized through the ideas of mysticism and alchemy. However, such ideas were discouraged by rational Enlightenment-era thinking. The ideas were only revived in the 19th century, in the United States and Europe, when an interest in the occult resurfaced. The Rosicrucian Fraternity in San Francisco, established by Pascal Beverly Randolph in 1858, was a nod to the legend of the Rosicrucians.

[
Johann Valentin Andreae is the author believed to have penned the mysterious pamphlets on the Rosicrucians. In his autobiography he confesses to writing *Chemical Wedding* but says it was never meant to be taken seriously.
]

Later, two popular 20th century societies, the Ancient Mystical Order Roase Crucis (AMORC) and The Rosicrucian Fellowship, reintroduced Rosicrucianism to the modern consciousness. AMORC founder Spencer Lewis sent mail-order lessons to attract new members, and with respect to the mystics who taught Christian Rosenkreuz, helped sponsor the Egypt Museum in San Jose, California. Meanwhile, the Seattle-based Rosicrucian Fellowship led to the creation of the Lectorium Rosicrucianum in the Netherlands.

THE ODD FELLOWS

THE FRIENDLIEST SOCIETY YOU'VE NEVER HEARD OF

The Odd Fellows is a worldwide society; its members are devoted to making charitable donations of time and money to their respective communities. The Odd Fellows originated in 14th-century England as a hodgepodge of guildsmen who did not have the experience or wealth to belong to "master" guilds. These guildsmen of disparate trades and specialties came together and formed the Odd Fellows, a charitable brotherhood whose members aided one another, their families, and communities in distress. In today's terms, the Odd Fellows was a pre-welfare organization. The group advocated for the impoverished and the ill, acting as an omnipresent friend to those in need.

The Odd Fellows stretched beyond England after the 14th century—a positive development for the poorer classes but not for the rich. Wealthy European aristocrats feared the coalition of working classes. Wealthy individuals were paranoid that the Odd Fellows would undermine governments, and in the 16th century the organization faced suppression by Pope Paul III and Queen Elizabeth I. Between the papacy and the British royalty, the Odd Fellows were left without infrastructure or rights to train apprentices. It only survived in England as a form of social support for its communities. Later, in 18th-century France, the noose around the Odd Fellows grew tighter as it was believed to have been behind a coup d'état staged against the French government. France passed a law banning the Odd Fellows, driving the community underground. The Freemasons were on the rise just as the Odd Fellows were pushed into obscurity.

> *The group advocated for the impoverished and the ill, acting as an omnipresent friend to those in need.*

I SAW THE SIGN

SIGNS AND SYMBOLS
OF SECRET SOCIETIES

Within every society are pictorial cues indicating something of significance to insiders. With a quick glance at a codified image, insiders can tap into a bit of information that helps fulfill a mission.

THE RED CROSS

Three major symbols were associated with the Knights Templar: one for battle and two for banking. While patrolling pilgrim routes or fighting armies, the Knights wore a white mantle with a red cross on their chests. Not to be confused with the Christian cross, the horizontal and vertical arms of the Knights Templar cross were equal in length. The society was formed in 1118, and its members began wearing the red cross in 1147 at the bequest of King Louis VII of France and Pope Eugenius III. Not only did

Above: Colored engraving of a Knight Templar in his war costume with his squire in 1255.

wearing the red cross help the Knights recognize one another from a distance, but it distinguished them to pilgrims, who might otherwise have been fooled into trusting imposters.

Today we immediately associate the red cross symbol with the International Committee of the Red Cross (ICRC), a humanitarian aid organization that provides relief to disaster-stricken communities worldwide. It is no coincidence that the ICRC symbol is almost identical to that of the Knights Templar. Jean Henri Dunant founded the ICRC in the mid-19th century. Dunant, a Freemason at the Knights Templar lodge, named after the original Knights Templar, who disbanded in the 14th century, had witnessed countless horrors in the aftermath of the Austro-Sardinian War at Solferino, Italy. Incredulous that injured soldiers were abandoned and left to care for themselves, he published *A Memory of Solferino* (1862), beseeching world leaders to take action on behalf of all people in need. The book's publication catalyzed a series of events that led to the founding of the International Red Cross in 1881. The red cross symbol was resurrected into public consciousness as a hallmark

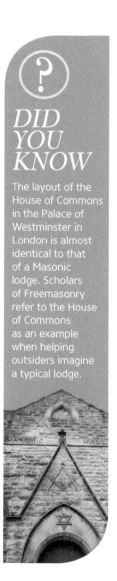

DID YOU KNOW

The layout of the House of Commons in the Palace of Westminster in London is almost identical to that of a Masonic lodge. Scholars of Freemasonry refer to the House of Commons as an example when helping outsiders imagine a typical lodge.

DEATH & TAXES

of support for those in need. Dunant was deeply influenced by the Knights Templar lodge and its admiration for the heroism of the original Knights Templar society, whose legendary gallantry had long been associated with the red cross symbol.

After the Knights Templar evolved into a hybrid fighting-banking society, it began using a double-sided seal on letters of credit in exchange for deposits. Other Knights Templar houses recognized these sealed letters, allowing those making deposits in one bank to withdraw funds wherever they traveled. One side of the seal depicted its headquarters at the Al-Aqsa Mosque with the Latin words *De Templo Cristi* (roughly translating to "The Temple of Christ"). The other side depicted two knights riding on one horse. Modern-day scholars believe the knights are Hugues de Payens and Godfrey de Saint-Omer, the founding members of the original order. If this theory is correct, they ride one horse as an indication of their poverty and humility. Around the circumference are the Latin words *Sigillum Militum Xpisti*, meaning "The Seal of a Soldier of Christ." The Knights Templar's banking system is often viewed as a precursor to modern-day banking, made possible by its creative use of symbols as a form of communication between Templar houses throughout the Middle East and Europe.

EXES AND EYES

Freemasonry is steeped in ritual and symbolism, perhaps more so than any other secret society in the world. Freemasonry evolved from a brotherhood of stonemasons who were never taught to read and write. Literacy rates were low among the tradesmen of 18th century Europe, and only the nobles owned books. People of the lower classes seldom knew how to write their own names, so stonemasons often employed the letter "X" as their signature, which became one of the early symbols synonymous with stonemasonry.

One of the most common symbols of Freemasonry is that of the Masonic square and compass, an illustration of a compass with its aperture open to 45 degrees enjoined with a ruler bent at a 90-degree angle. These are the prosaic tools of the stonemason and architect, whose work is revered by modern-day Freemasons, many of whom are far removed from construction and engineering work. *Duncan's Masonic Ritual and Monitor* (1866) says the orthogonal ruler represents the "squaring" of a mason's actions, while the compass reminds him to stay "within bounds with all mankind." Many lodges include a capital "G" in the empty space between the compass and ruler. Depending on the lodge, this "G" can represent either God or geometry, both objects of veneration in Freemasonry.

The Eye of Providence is another essential Masonic symbol—one that we see every day in the United States. The symbol is an image of a disembodied eye with rays of light emanating from behind. The *Freemason's Monitor* (1797), by Thomas Smith Webb, calls it a reminder of God's ubiquitous presence. While the eye resonates with Freemasons as part of their Masonic rituals, it reminds most Americans of the dollar bill. The eye can be found on the back of our smallest paper unit of currency, floating above an unfinished pyramid. It comes as no surprise that a committee of Freemasons designed the seal. The unfinished pyramid beneath the eye was a last-minute addition, likely at the suggestion of Thomas Jefferson, a one-time member of the Bavarian Illuminati. The seal was adopted by Congress in 1782 and was placed on the reverse of the US one-dollar bill in 1935, under the administration of a Freemason, President Franklin Roosevelt.

THE UBIQUITOUS OWL

One symbol that has withstood both the passage of time and the disbanding of the Bavarian Illuminati is the Owl of Minerva, seen in many 18th-century Bavarian Illuminati seals. The owl represents the Roman goddess of wisdom, Minerva (known as Athena in Greek mythology). Today the owl can be spotted (with the help of a magnifying glass) on the front of the US one-dollar bill, perched on the left side of the upper-left number "1."

In contrast to the founders of Freemasonry, the founders of the Bavarian Illuminati were intellectuals. Weishaupt was a professor, and those who joined him were literate upper-class men, duly capable of communicating through writing. However, to keep their activities a secret, the Bavarian Illuminati communicated via codified images. One of their most important symbols was an unfinished pyramid depicted on the carpet of their meeting room at the Minerval Church. Flanking either

Masonic symbols in Gloucester Cathedral in Britain.

side of the design were the letters "D" and "P," representing the Latin phrase *Deo Proximo*, or "God Is Near." The incipient pyramid is a reminder that God's work is not yet done. The same unfinished pyramid stands below the floating Eye of Providence on the reverse of the US one-dollar bill. According to Secretary of Agriculture Henry A. Wallace, President Franklin Roosevelt resurrected the seal designed by the founding fathers because the unfinished pyramid resonated with him. Wallace said it reflected Roosevelt's notion that the country could only be completed "under the eye of the Great Architect."

ROC-A-FELLA DIAMOND

According to conspiracy theorists David Icke and Alex Jones, celebrities tend to give clues that they belong to the Illuminati. One clue is the "Roc-A-Fella Diamond," a hand gesture originated by rapper Shawn "Jay-Z" Carter. In 1995, Jay-Z, along with Damon Dash and Kareem Burke, founded Roc-A-Fella Records, and the "Roc-A-Fella diamond" hand sign is a signature of the label. Jay-Z, his wife, Beyoncé Knowles-Carter, and those signed with Roc-A-Fella (including Kanye West, Cam'ron, and Jadakiss) flash the sign of the diamond in music videos, concerts, and photographs. The record label is associated with the infamous Rockefeller family through Comcast Corporation.

Conspiracy theories assert that the overarching wealth and avarice of the Rockefellers make them obvious Illuminati conspirators. All companies associated with the Rockefellers are thereby up for speculation, including Roc-A-Fella Records. Because the triangular shape of the Roc-A-Fella diamond is reminiscent of the Bavarian Illuminati pyramid on the one-dollar bill, some view it as a message that Roc-A-Fella Records is a constituent of the Illuminati. By that reasoning, Jay-Z's involvement is demonstrated when he makes the diamond sign over his left eye, suggesting his is the Eye of Providence.

SING IT!

IN 1995, *The Simpsons* was nominated for an Emmy Award in Outstanding Individual Achievement in Music and Lyrics with the song "We Do," featured in the episode "Homer the Great." The episode is replete with references to the Freemasons, *Indiana Jones: Raiders of the Lost Ark* (1981), the Ark of the Covenant, and the *Last Emperor* (1987). In the song "We Do," the "Stonecutters" (*The Simpsons'* version of the Freemasons) sing proudly about being the powerful elite who control the government, media, and systems of measurement. Through the song, *Simpsons* creator Matthew Groening vented his frustration with what he believes are misconceptions about the Freemasons ruling the world.

THE TOP 10

MOST EXTREME MEMBERSHIP REQUIREMENTS

1 The Skoptsy of Russia A small Siberian society of 100 people, the Skoptsy's initiation rites include castration and removing the breasts. Andrei Ivanov and Kondratii Selivanov began the society in the mid-18th century as a way to rid Christians of the "imperfections" of the human body. The Skoptsy believe that one can only live a "perfect life" by removing the sex organs. Selivanov preached his beliefs on the streets of St. Petersburg, claiming he was the reincarnation of Tsar Peter III.

2 Leopard Society The Leopard Society of West Africa was a highly dangerous group of cannibals who dressed in leopard skins, cat teeth, and sharp metal claws before going on killing sprees in the jungle. They ambushed their victims and mauled them to death. They drained the victims' blood into vials and drank it for its purported ability to give them "supernatural powers." The society ran rampant in Sierra Leone and Nigeria after World War I, and it wasn't until 1948 that the government and civilians apprehended and imprisoned them all.

3 Scientology The Rundown is a rigorous and costly "spiritual" practice of detoxifying the body during which former drug users spend five weeks following a "purification" program of jogging in rubber suits, steaming in saunas for five hours a day, and consuming high doses of niacin. At the start of the program, niacin doses are almost six times the medically recommended dose. By the end of the five weeks, people are administered 5,000 milligrams of niacin per day—more than 333 times the medically recommended dose.

4 Aghori Babas The Aghori Babas of India have long been known to eat the dead. This necrophagic group believes that by consuming human flesh, they will no longer fear death but will attain spiritual enlightenment. Because the Hindu majority in India cremate their dead, the Aghori Babas wait at the banks of the Ganges River for those who are not allowed to be cremated, namely pregnant women, children, unmarried women, and holy men.

5 Yanomami This Amazon rainforest–dwelling group views death as an unnatural phenomenon, believing it to be caused by malevolent shamans from warring tribes. Yanomami cremate the body, thereby liberating the spirit, and mix the ashes with fermented banana. They consume the mixture to assure that the soul of the deceased lives on through them.

6 Vodun A religious group in West Africa who believe that through ritual fasting they become vessels for the earth spirit Sakpata, Vodun's rituals involve abandoning initiates in a forest for three days without food or drink. The person is weakened, eventually losing consciousness to connect with Sakpata. A second set of rituals is performed after the fast to revive the person's strength.

7 Kaningara In Papua New Guinea, a group called the Kaningara practices ritual body modification on adolescents to strengthen the children's spiritual connection with the environment. The ritual begins with the child living in seclusion for 60 days in the Haus Tambaran ("The Spirit House"). Afterward, the adults make deep cuts all over the initiate's body, leaving the child's skin to look as though it's been chewed by a crocodile. To the Kaningara, crocodiles are the gods who create humans. In marking an adolescent to look like he has been eaten and expelled by a crocodile, the elders make them look as though they were consumed as children and regurgitated as adults.

9 **The Light** A Manhattan-based cult called The Light has made headlines for using corporal punishment as a way to "treat" homosexuality, officially banned within the organization. Gay men are forced to accustom themselves to heterosexual relationships and are set up to marry female members of the cult. The Light, believing the end of the world is just around the corner, forces men to undergo weapons training to prepare for war on doomsday.

8 **The Order of the Peacock Angel** This British group is rooted in the beliefs of the Yazidis of the Middle East and worships the Peacock Angel. The order believes peacocks can answer prayers, and they worship at the altar of live peacocks. Members dance slowly and methodically around the altar while making silent wishes to the birds. The dance takes on speed and builds into a frenzy, after which everyone falls down in ecstasy.

10 **The Secte Rouge** Author Zora Neale Hurston was the first to write about the Secte Rouge, a Haitian society that robs graves and eats decomposed corpses. The Secte Rouge was known to abduct and cannibalize children. Hurston's neighbors warned her that the Secte Rouge view travelers as "special delicacies."

NIGHTS OF RITES

ENTER IN SECRET, STAY IN SECRET

For most secret societies, an initiation ceremony marks new members' entry into the group. These ceremonies are important not only for the initiate, but also for the entire group. By partaking in ritual initiations, new members demonstrate their seriousness and loyalty to the group. In turn, the group earns the trust of new members. The initiation ritual is often the first in a series, with successive ceremonies allowing members access to higher degrees of knowledge, power, and responsibility.

The Knights Templar had a very well-documented initiation ceremony. To ordain with the order, one had to be in excellent health, unmarried, and without debt. Once all this was verified, the initiate went to one of the Templar's domed churches (all built to resemble the Holy Sepulchre, a church built on the site where Jesus is thought to have died) for the ceremony. Knights Templar ceremonies began under the dome with the master knight giving the knights an opportunity to reject the initiate immediately; one objection was enough to boot a potential Templar. If the initiate passed, he went to an adjoining room where three senior knights explained the difficulties of being in the order, as well as their expectations of the possible knight-to-be. If the initiate still desired to be a knight after hearing what

Left: Future members of an English Freemasonry lodge being guided with their eyes covered during their initiation, around 1933.

was expected of him, he returned to the main room and was asked again by the master knight if he was willing to sacrifice his former life for the challenging life of a Templar. Other knights were also allowed to ask the initiate questions. If the initiate survived the questioning, he was sworn in. In taking the oath, the new knight promised to remain a Templar for life and keep the order's secrets to himself. Afterward, the knight was granted a woven belt and the Templar uniform called the tabard of the Knights Templar. Finally, the Master Knight gave the new knight a kiss on the lips, neck, and midsection to consummate the ceremony.

Not all initiation ceremonies are as serious as that of the Knights Templar. Initiation at the Bohemian Grove is treated like the kickoff at the Super Bowl. Because the society only gathers once a year for a three-week camping retreat, it holds an initiation ceremony for everyone on the first Saturday of the retreat. In this

. . . .

✳ **Duncan's Masonic Ritual and Monitor** (1866), by Malcolm C. Duncan, provides detailed illustrations and descriptions of Masonic symbols and rituals from the York Rite of Freemasonry, a high-level Masonic order dealing specifically with symbols, rituals, and cryptic messages.

. . . .

ceremony, called the Cremation of Care, members dress in robes and burn a fake corpse before a 40-foot statue of an owl. The corpse represents "Care," as in the cares of the world. Once the corpse turns to dust, everyone is initiated and society activities can officially commence.

Throughout society, rites of passage or initiation that are celebrated draw less than a moment's thought. Weddings and school graduations are common American ceremonies. Social privilege is formally recognized in school graduations, which not only honor the graduate's work at the school but mark the right to advance to successive levels of education. The cap-and-gown attire at school graduations is reminiscent of the long monochromatic robes worn at the Bohemian Grove. Like the Care of Cremation ceremony, graduations appeal to a mass of people rather than a single initiate and are typically followed by celebration.

PRESIDENTS IN SECRET SOCIETIES

THE RED, WHITE, AND WHO?

FREEMASONS

George Washington · James Monroe · Andrew Jackson · James Polk · James Buchanan · Andrew Johnson · James Garfield · William McKinley · Theodore Roosevelt · Howard Taft · Warren Harding · Franklin Roosevelt · Harry Truman · Gerald Ford

SKULL AND BONES

William Howard Taft · George H. W. Bush · George W. Bush

WHAT EVIL LURKS IN THE HEARTS OF MEN?

HISTORY IS FULL OF SOCIETIES BUILT ON HATRED AND CRUELTY

"There is power in unity and there is power in numbers," Martin Luther King Jr. said in his "Keep on Moving" speech in May 1963. These words resonate today, as seen in the #BlackLivesMatter movement and the protests in Ferguson, Missouri, in 2014. We see the truth of "power in numbers" as it manifests among peaceful protesters, but also violently in groups propagating terror and tyranny. Some groups choose secrecy to keep their business private, while others choose anonymity with the explicit purpose of making their crimes (but

Right: A Ku Klux Klan cross burns at the bicentennial celebration, Pulaski, Tennessee, May 31, 1976.

A Ku Klux Klan member demonstrates the ritualistic aspects of a KKK meeting.

not their criminals) public, using them as scare tactics to harass, intimidate, and harm people—people whose race tends to differ from that of the aggressors.

THE THULE SOCIETY

The Thule Society of early-20th-century Germany drew sharp criticism for its grandiose ideals of world domination and Satanic ritual. It's sometimes blamed for thrusting Adolf Hitler into power and dreaming up the Third Reich—a theoretical thousand-year Aryan occupation of planet Earth. Originally founded as a study group in 1911, the Thule Society quickly became a cover group for the unpopular Germanenorden, a secret order of occultists who inculcated initiates with ideas of Aryan superiority and anti-Semitism. Upon swearing into the society, initiates signed the "blood declaration of faith," stating they had no bloodline relationship to non-Aryan people, namely Jews and people of color.

The Thule Society began influencing public opinion with its purchase of the *Munich Observer*, a weekly newspaper that became the *People's Observer*, the main source of Nazi news in Germany. Thule member Karl Harrer edited the paper, and in 1919 made fast friends with the influential right-wing politician Anton Drexler. Together Harrer and Drexler established the German Worker's Party (*Deutsche Arbeiterpartei*, or DAP), a political group whose aims were racial purity and the extermination of all threats to the Aryan bloodline. One of the DAP's early members was a German nationalist and failed art student by the name of Adolf Hitler. Hitler had been known to give grandiloquent street speeches about the Jews' culpability in the dismal state of postwar Germany and was swiftly gaining a following among the masses of hungry, impoverished, disillusioned Germans. Between these speeches and the articles published in the *Munich Observer*, early-20th-century Germany was inundated with anti-Semitic rhetoric. With the benefit of hindsight, it is easy to see how Hitler won the 1939 election for German chancellor in a landslide.

If the Nazi Party was a forest fire, the Thule Society was the match and kerosene that set it ablaze. In the seven years the Thule Society operated, 1918 to 1925, it systematically inspired hatred in the hearts and minds of the German people, though

Hitler himself was not a member. His connection to the society was through Thule member Dietrich Eckhart, who reluctantly agreed to attend one of Hitler's bombastic street speeches, only to leave the speech utterly inspired. Eckhart instantly knew he had found a leader in Hitler and that it was his life's mission to coach Hitler for the sake of the Third Reich. Under the tutelage of Eckhart, Hitler became a powerful orator and prominent figure in Germany. The two shared an intimate teacher-apprentice bond until Eckhart's death in 1923. Hitler dedicated his 1926 autobiographical manifesto *Mein Kampf* to Eckhart.

THE KU KLUX KLAN

The Ku Klux Klan is the most-talked-about hate-mongering group in American history. The Klan promotes the so-called "purity" of the Caucasian race and is vocal about its hatred for other racial, ethnic, and religious groups. The primary targets of its invective are African Americans, Jewish people, and gays and lesbians. Since the Klan's founding, it has terrorized the public, and over the course of 150 years it has infiltrated American politics with agendas of racial segregation and oppression. Even with a 40-year hiatus between 1876 and 1915, the Klan managed to amass a following of 4 million people in 1921. Although it fell out of favor in the 1970s, there are an estimated 5,000 to 6,000 Klan members in the United States as of 2015.

The American South was in deep economic despair after the Civil War. Not only had the war been costly in terms of lives and resources, but it created a paradigm shift that the Confederacy fought desperately to avoid. From this despondent state of affairs came the Ku Klux Klan, a six-member fraternal organization of college-educated war veterans. In a bar in Pulaski, Tennessee, in 1865, the men decided to form a group and give themselves a Greek name. They chose the Greek word for "circle" *(keu klos)*, changed it to "ku klux," and added the word "klan" at the end to create what would become one of the most infamous names in American history. At first, Klan members only focused on entertaining themselves, bestowing upon one another titles like "Grand Cyclops" and "Grand Magi." They disguised themselves in white sheets, thrilled by the notion that people thought they were ghoulish and scary, and rode their horses through town.

Shortly after the founding of the Ku Klux Klan, the South began to feel the pinch of the Reconstruction Era. Republicans had passed the Reconstruction Act of 1867, granting African Americans suffrage and dividing the South into 50 small military-controlled districts. This fundamental change in the social order of the South was not well received, and white supremacists decided to take action. By then, the Klansmen had ballooned in number, rising to the forefront of vigilantism for white supremacy. They terrorized African American voters on election days,

SUPREME RECANT

Hugo Black was a Klansman and US Senator from Alabama from 1927 to 1937. He later recanted his support for the Ku Klux Klan when he was nominated for Supreme Court Justice during the Roosevelt administration. Black served on the Supreme Court from 1937 to 1971.

DID YOU KNOW

President Woodrow Wilson screened *The Birth of a Nation* in the White House and called the Ku Klux Klan a "heroic force." He reportedly said the only bad part of the movie was that it was "so terribly true."

savagely beating and hanging them as they approached the polls. Warnings were left on the doors of African American homes, threatening violence if their inhabitants attempted to vote.

The Klan was subdued for a time by the Enforcement Act and Ku Klux Klan Act of 1871, making it a federal crime for two or more people to conspire or disguise themselves with the intent of denying anyone their civil rights. The Klan went quiet for roughly 40 years. Then, in 1915, a movie was released that thrust the Ku Klux Klan back into the American spotlight. *The Birth of a Nation,* a D. W. Griffith film, reignited the flame of virulent racism. *Nation* was set during the Civil War and told the story of two families, one pro-Union, the other pro-Confederacy. The film portrays black men as savage brutes who attack white women. The protagonists of the story are the Klansmen, who

In 2005 the US Supreme Court ruled in favor of the Klan participating in Missouri's adopt-a-highway program, claiming that denying their application infringed upon their First Amendment rights. Missouri later renamed the KKK-adopted highway after civil rights activist Rosa Parks.

triumphantly suppress black suffrage by the end of the film. In the final scene, Jesus and his angels are depicted amid a crowd of cheering white people, demonstrating their silent approval of the Klansmen. White supremacists across the country lauded the film, which inspired a revival of the Ku Klux Klan, with Methodist preacher-turned-salesman William T. Simmons as its founder and leader.

Klan hatred took on a greater magnitude in its new incarnation. This time, it gave money to Protestant churches and made patriotism one of its rallying cries. "One-hundred-percent Americanism" was its slogan, and this time the Klan included Jews, Catholics, and immigrants with African Americans on its list of people to hate. By 1921, within only 15 months of its refounding, the Klan had swelled to 100,000 members. Congress initially scheduled hearings to address the Klan's misappropriation of donations received from new members. It seemed the country was taking a stand for African Americans and that Klan terror would soon end. At the first and only hearing, Simmons used his spurious charm to dazzle Congress and garner support for the Klan. In the decades to come, the Ku Klux Klan infiltrated city and state governments from New Jersey to California. Between threats and intimidation at the polls, and strong financial backing from wealthy donors and illegal business transactions, the Klan helped elect 16 Klan sympathizers to the Senate, five of whom were Klan members themselves.

The Ku Klux Klan was extra vigilant during the civil rights movement. The Klan stymied African American architectural and engineering efforts and bombed homes, killing whomever happened to be there. In Birmingham, Alabama, they were supported by police commissioner Bull Conner, who allowed the Klan 15 minutes to attack the Freedom Riders, a group of racially integrated civil rights activists who opposed segregation by riding buses together throughout the country. This was one of many transgressions that led the federal government to intervene in local politics. By 1964 the Civil Rights Act and subsequent legislation was passed to protect the voting and civil rights of African Americans. This victory for equality was a major setback for the Klan, which redirected its focus on open immigration and resegregating schools.

Today's Klan exists as nine small chapters, with the majority of members in the South and about a third in the Midwest. It is decreasing in popularity and size every year. In 2012 alone, the Ku Klux Klan lost one-third of its membership. Most Klan campaigning focuses on oppressing same-sex marriage equality and countering illegal immigration. At times, the American Civil Liberties Union (ACLU) has provided the Klan legal support in defense of its freedom of speech, which has been challenged on a number of occasions by groups and individuals who don't want the Klan infiltrating their communities.

BANNED
MEETING LIST

ROLLING OUT THE UNWELCOME MAT

Many of the world's secret societies operate outside the law. Some nations explicitly ban these societies from gathering, while others refuse to cave to their requests for credence.

SCIENTOLOGY
- considered a cult in Chile
- denied approval as a religion in Denmark and France
- fined $900,000 by France in 2009 for allegations of fraud

FREEMASONRY
- illegal in China and Iran, which had 43 Masonic lodges before the 1979 Islamic Revolution

KU KLUX KLAN
- notorious Klansman David Duke was expelled from Italy in 2013 and banned from returning for attempting to start a faction there

ORIGINS

Where and when did the main secret societies begin?
The creation of these groups span both the globe
and the centuries.

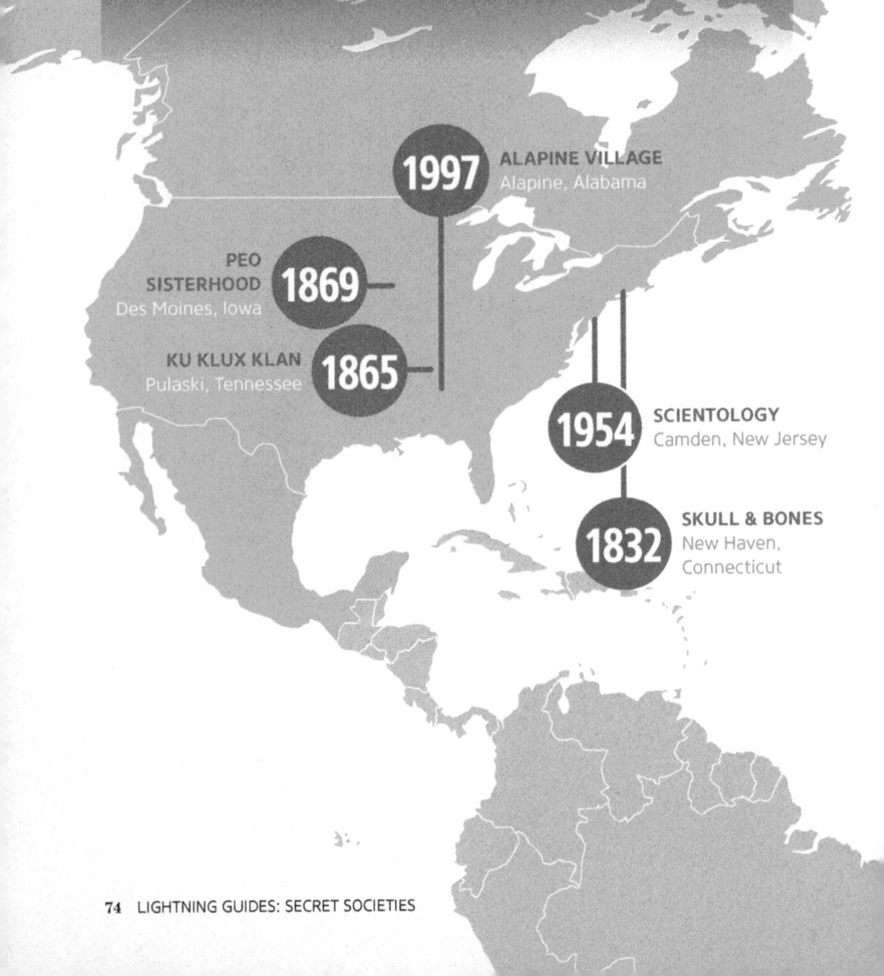

1997
ALAPINE VILLAGE
Alapine, Alabama

PEO
SISTERHOOD
Des Moines, Iowa
1869

KU KLUX KLAN
Pulaski, Tennessee
1865

1954
SCIENTOLOGY
Camden, New Jersey

1832
SKULL & BONES
New Haven,
Connecticut

THULE SOCIETY
Berlin
1918

FREEMASONS
London
1717

BAVARIAN
ILLUMINATI
Ingolstadt, Bavaria
1776

BILDERBERG GROUP
Oosterbeek, Netherlands
1954

KNIGHTS TEMPLAR
Jerusalem
1119
AD

WHERE ARE THE WOMEN?

FEMALE SECRET SOCIETIES OF THE WORLD

Secret societies exclusive to women are far less common than fraternal organizations, but they do exist. Women have been involved in Freemasonry since 1850 with the Order of the Eastern Star, and on a more sinister note, there were female Ku Klux Klan organizations in the 1920s. Matriarchal societies are uncommon, but there are a few. The history and activities of women-only secret societies are not unlike those of male societies. There is a desire to bond around secrets only privy to those on the inside. In the case of female societies, there is often a barrier of oppression when women assert themselves within a larger patriarchal society.

THE WOMEN OF THE KLAN

The Women's Ku Klux Klan (WKKK) was inspired by the Klan's revival after the 1915 debut of *The Birth of a Nation*. Coinciding with second-wave feminism, female sympathizers of the

Left: Joan of Arc, the Maid of Orléans, national heroine of France and a Roman Catholic saint.

Ku Klux Klan were anxious to assist in oppressing racial and religious minorities in America. Their first chapter formed in 1923 in Little Rock, Arkansas, and by 1925 there were 4 million WKKK members representing all US states. Only white Protestant women over the age of 16 were allowed entry into the WKKK. Recruitment was solicited through advertisements with rhetoric about "restoring America" and preserving the white race. Klanswomen's activities included organizing festivals, parades, and rallies; cross-burnings; and boycotts. Like the KKK, they held rites of passage such as Klan weddings, christenings, and funerals.

Unlike the KKK, the WKKK advocated for white supremacy almost exclusively through politics. It sought to change everyday life without the use of physical force or violence. The women didn't have anything against violence per se, but they did not use it as their primary method of affecting change. The WKKK did not last long. Although the group was widespread by the late 1920s, it was rife with corruption and scandal. The WKKK disbanded, and women were unheard of in Klan activities until the end of second-wave feminism in the 1980s. Participation in the KKK is now open to women, and there have been female Klan leaders.

ORDER OF THE EASTERN STAR

Freemason and educator Rob Morris established the Order of the Eastern Star in 1850 as a form of Freemasonry open to men and women over the age of 18. Morris was inspired during a bout of illness to start a unisex lodge, and he wrote the principles of the lodge in *Rosary of the Eastern Star,* changed to *Ritual of the Order of the Eastern Star* in 1866. The only stipulation for female members was that they must have had a legal or bloodline relationship to a master Mason. In 1876, the general grand chapter of the Eastern Star was formed in Indiana. The principles of the order have remained relatively unchanged. Today, the Order of the Eastern Star has chapters in 20 countries, with about 500,000 members.

The Order of the Eastern Star reveres women in the Bible and teaches the stories of Ruth, Esther, Martha (Mary's sister), Adah (from the Book of Judges), and Electa (from the Second Epistle of John) to instill the values of faith and perseverance in lodge members. As a way to honor these biblical characters, the order has used their names as titles for its members. For instance, an "Esther" is entrusted with sharing the value of loyalty with her friends and family. A "Ruth" shares honor and justice, and an "Adah" shares the lesson of obeying God. These titles, along with matron, conductress, and associate conductress, can be held only by women. One of the most important aspects of this lodge is philanthropy: The Order of the Eastern Star makes major contributions to Alzheimer's research, and gives scholarships to students of religious music and theology.

BETTY THE BUILDER

The Alapine Village pioneers created the community's infrastructure from nothing. They set up electricity and water pipelines and laid paved roads along the 400-acre property in rural Alabama —a road that today's women of the Alapine use in their everyday lives.

Women's Christian Temperance Union (WCTU) members singing "Dry, Clean California." The WCTU was aided in its efforts by the International Organization of Good Templars, a fraternal organization modeled on Freemasonry which works to reduce harm caused by alcohol and other drugs.

THE PEO SISTERHOOD

The PEO Sisterhood is a women's society focusing on educating female students everywhere. There are 250,000 PEO members worldwide, and the organization is headquartered in Des Moines, Iowa. The society opened in the mid-19th century as a network of Methodist women's colleges and became international in 1911 with the founding of the Vancouver chapter. By then it had become a community-based organization, modest in its scale of work. The activities of the PEO were understated until 2005, when it launched a campaign called "It's OK to Talk About PEO." On Founder's Day that year, a PEO logo was introduced to the once highly secretive organization.

As of 2014, the PEO Sisterhood had made education possible for 90,000 women and contributed more than $200 million to female education. PEO has an educational loan fund and is the supervising authority over the all-women's Cottey College and the International Peace Scholarship Fund. Through this fund, women in 174 countries around the world can be subsidized for graduate-level education. Despite the organization's prominence and seeming transparency, the PEO still retains secrets at the upper echelons. Outsiders do not know conclusively what PEO stands for; its website claims it stands for Philanthropic Educational Organization, but this is up for speculation. All PEO meetings are private and by invitation only. Insiders say they open with inspirational readings and prayer but are nondenominational.

ALAPINE VILLAGE

A small community of women began Alapine Village in 1997. A rural community for lesbian women who pride themselves on building their own homes, tending to farms, and structuring their own social order, Alapine is highly selective about its membership. The group is strict about only admitting lesbian women, at the exclusion of bisexual and transsexual women. The society does not share its activities with the outside world, preferring to operate in secret. The women enjoy spending time in nature,

making art, gardening, and playing music, and they want peace and privacy. "I came here because I wanted to be in nature, and I wanted to have lesbian neighbors," said 62-year-old pioneer Emily Greene in a rare article with the *New York Times* in 2009 titled "My Sister's Keeper."

Alapine Village community members were explicit in their distaste for men. They did not like living in the confines of the larger patriarchal American society, which oppressed many of the pioneers in their young adult years. Barbara Moore was in the military when she came out as a lesbian in the 1960s, and in a 2009 *New York Times* article she described the reaction as a "witch hunt." Her wife and co-pioneer, Winnie Adams, also described a frustrating experience living in the 1950s and 1960s. "I did everything I was supposed to do," she said. "I went to college, I got my job, I got my man, I got my two kids. But it still didn't feel right."

> **1869** The first PEO Sisterhood was founded by seven women at Iowa Wesleyan College. They became the second sorority in the United States. Oil portraits by Mario Dunlap Harper depict some of the women wearing their sorority apparel—a red hooded cape.

Phi Tau group portrait, circa 1908. Early all-female fraternal organizations modeled themselves after their male counterparts, including the use of secret rituals and mottoes.

Like her co-pioneers and the women who came after her, Adams found solace, friendship, and acceptance at Alapine Village. The community, while dwindling in numbers in the early 2000s, made a comeback after the *New York Times* article. The 13-member Alapine Village received donations and lesbian visitors from around the country in a "whirlwind of activity" (as described on their website, Alapine.org).

MATRIARCHIES OF THE WORLD

THOUGH NOT SECRET, THESE WOMEN-CENTERED SOCIETIES ARE RELATIVELY UNKNOWN

The Ede In the Ede villages of Vietnam, women propose marriage to men, own all the family property, and pass it on to their daughters before they die. Men take their wife's surname and move into her family's house after marriage. The society is the inverse of most, except its members don't believe in owning land outside their own homes. To the Ede, the villages are communal and the forests belong to no one.

The Mosuo Among the Mosuo of China, women take the reins in business affairs. The family leader, called the Ah Mi, is the eldest female in the household. All families share communal spaces, except for women over the age of 13, who are given their own bedroom in which to "flower." Women are also allowed to see other men while they're married, while men are expected to remain faithful to their wives.

The Chambri In Papua New Guinea, the Chambri society puts women in charge of providing for the family—and the community at large. Women fish for their families and are given the upper hand in making political decisions. The Chambri inspired first-wave feminism in the United States when Margaret Mead wrote about her visit with them in the 1930s.

The Meghalaya Meghalaya, India (pictured at left), is officially the rainiest place in the world and is a matriarchal society where only women own property and land. The youngest daughter inherits land from her mother and is responsible for her unwed siblings and aging parents. In modern times, men have been rallying for civil rights, disturbed by how the society undercuts male potential and drives them to seek solace in drugs and alcohol.

THE NEWBIES

SECRET SOCIETIES OF THE 20TH CENTURY

I t might be easy to understand the formation of secret societies centuries ago—when social norms strictly suppressed individual expression—but what role do secret societies have today? With the rise of widespread literacy and democracy, what has inspired the foundation of modern secretive groups?

ORDO TEMPLI ORIENTIS

The Ordo Templi Orientis (OTO) was established at the turn of the 20th century in Austria by Carl Kellner, a scientist, inventor,

Above: An artist's rendition of the assassination of Archduke Franz Ferdinand of Austria-Hungary and his wife by Serbian nationalist Gavrilo Princip, a member of the Black Hand.

and industrialist, and Theodor Reuss, a German occultist and Freemason. Kellner and Reuss had a vision for an occult Masonry, a rarity among lodges at the time. In 1904, Reuss garnered authority to perform the Masonic Rite of Memphis-Misraïm, effectively granting him and Kellner Freemason status for their order. The men had envisioned an organization modeled after European Freemasonry, but their plans changed when a man named Aleister Crowley joined the order. Crowley, a self-proclaimed prophet who purported to lead humanity into its next phase of spiritual development, called the "Aeon of Horus," was admitted to the OTO by Reuss in 1910. In four years, Crowley advanced to a tenth-degree member and had brought OTO to Ireland, Britain, Russia, and the United States. He had also composed a Gnostic mass for the group, written a manifesto (the Mysteria Mystica Maxima), and integrated the Law of Thelema into the OTO belief system. By 1920, Crowley had single-handedly revised the order's beliefs, rituals, and hierarchical structure. In 1925, Crowley ascended to the highest position of authority in OTO, outer head of the order (OHO), where he remained until

FIRST BASE

"Sex magic" is the primary lesson at the hermit level of OTO. Hermits are taught "magical masturbation." Once a hermit has demonstrated their competency with this lesson, they move on to the magical techniques of vaginal and anal intercourse.

his death in 1947. The OTO remains a worldwide organization with an international headquarters overseeing all operations. Grand lodges function at the national level in all countries with an OTO presence.

OTO is best known for its fervent religiosity. The society is steeped in dramatic ritual, which conveys spiritual teachings to its members. Ritual activity in OTO is either centered on the mysteries of life and the universe or the Gnostic mass itself. Crowley wrote that the second main objective of the rituals was to "instruct every man (and woman) how to best adapt his (or her) life to the cosmos and to develop his or her faculties to the utmost advantage." The 13 degrees of the order are conferred through ceremonies and are divided into hermits, lovers, and men of Earth. The lessons of ritualistic OTO ceremonies depend on the level to which one ascends. The ultimate lesson of OTO is for the practitioner to fully discover him or herself. In addition to the rituals, wisdom is imparted to members via lectures, social events, classes, books, and art exhibits. The OTO urges initiates to realize the divinity of humanity and to follow the illuminated ethical principles set forth by Crowley in the *Book of the Law*. According to the book, the OTO values loyalty, courage, discretion, skepticism, and independence above all else.

THE BLACK HAND

Perhaps the most volatile of the shorter-lived secret societies was the Black Hand, a group of Serbian terrorists credited with the assassination of Archduke Franz Ferdinand in the July Crisis of 1914, which ignited World War I, severing long-standing ties among imperial allies and ultimately savaging Europe.

The Black Hand was originally formed by a group of Serbian army men on October 8, 1908, under the name National Defense. The Austro-Hungarian Empire had annexed Bosnia and Herzegovina days earlier, a haughty move that infuriated the Serbian nationalists of the National Defense. These men had enough of the ever-expanding empire and its influence on Serbian identity, and they formed a united albeit clandestine front for ripping the empire asunder. They launched an anti-Austrian propaganda campaign and trained spies to gather information for their eventual coup d'état. National Defense grew underground at a rapid pace and had satellite branches in Bosnia, Herzegovina, Slovenia, and Istria. On September 6, 1911, National Defense joined forces with a little-known group called the Black Hand, which had impressed the underground by assassinating Serbian King Alexander I and Queen Draga in May 1903. The new organization established the Unification or Death, a pact that swore all members would fulfill the purpose of unifying the Southern Slavic states or die trying.

Members of the original Black Hand undertook most of the group's terrorist activities, while other members continued influencing the Serbian consciousness via anti-Austrian propaganda and leading intelligence operations. The Black Hand was effective because many members held positions in the Serbian army and government. The group had friends in high places, including Crown Prince Alexander, who financed terrorist

"The Law of Thelema," written by Aleister Crowley, is the spiritual foundation of the OTO. It decrees, "Do what thou wilt shall be the whole of the Law. Love is the law, love under will." Crowley published it in his *Book of Law*. He claimed to have channeled the information in the book from an incorporeal entity named Aiwass.

operations with imperial money. The Black Hand was not to be crossed. The group enlisted three young Bosnian terrorists to murder Archduke Franz Ferdinand on his visit to Sarajevo. Roughly a month after the killing, Serbia was invaded by both Austria-Hungary and Germany.

The Serbian prime minister took initiative to dissolve the Black Hand in 1916, and by 1917, four high-ranking members of the group were arrested. The men were tried in the Salonika Trial, convicted of crimes against Serbia, and executed by firing squad on June 26, 1917. With these executions, the Black Hand was obliterated from the political stage.

THE BILDERBERG GROUP

The Bilderberg Group is the most clandestine society that has come to light. From what few accounts there are, the group consists of about 150 of the world's top leaders from every major industry. Members meet once a year for a weekend in a hotel, usually in Europe, and have never allowed the media into their meetings. Nobody from the outside has ever successfully infiltrated the group. The first meeting was on May 31, 1954, at the Hotel de Bilderberg in the Netherlands—thus the name, given to them by outsiders. Nobody knows what the members initially called themselves. The meeting was held to address the anti-American sentiment pervading Western Europe, and Prince Bernhard of the Netherlands initiated the meeting. Eleven countries were represented, including the United States. Participants found it so successful that they decided to meet every year.

Over time, the meetings began to take structure. According to American Friends of Bilderberg, a supposed link to the inside, the

Hotel Suvretta in St. Moritz, Switzerland, venue of the Bilderberg Club meeting on June 9, 2011.

meetings are arranged by a steering committee consisting of two members from each of the countries represented that year. There are advisers, chairmen, and an honorary secretary general. The Dutch economist Ernst van der Beugel was appointed permanent secretary in 1960. He was succeeded by Joseph Johnson of the Carnegie Endowment, CIA analyst William Bundy, who served as foreign affair adviser to US presidents John F. Kennedy and Lyndon B. Johnson, and former US ambassador to Afghanistan Theodore L. Eliot. The American Friends of Bilderberg claim that the meetings are the group's only activity. They say that nothing officially happens as a result of the meetings, but that account is questionable because the American Friends, including David Rockefeller and Henry Kissinger, are likely to have been Bilderberg Group participants themselves.

BUGGY BUNCH

Cicada 3301 puzzles were so challenging, even in terms of trying to decide what they were asking, that the US Navy and the National Security Agency used them as a model for their 2014 recruitment puzzles.

Because of its high-profile participant list, the Bilderberg Group has been accused of conspiring against the masses. Left-wing political theorists say the group is planning to impose a capitalist world government, while right-wing theorists accuse them of planning a one-world government. The one-world government accusation is similar to charges laid against the Illuminati. Former Bilderberg Group participant and British Secretary of State for Defense from 1964 to 1970 Denis Healey lent credence to some of these ideas when he said, "To say we were striving for a one-world government is exaggerated but not wholly unfair. Those of us in Bilderberg felt we couldn't go on forever fighting one another for nothing and killing people and rendering millions homeless. So we felt that a single community throughout the world would be a good thing." Whether the aims of the group are so innocent is an open question.

The Illuminati (2004), by Larry Burkett, is a science fiction novel set in 2020, when the United States elects a member of the Illuminati for president. The president launches a financial system called Data-Net, which controls personal finances and economies worldwide.

CICADA 3301

The secret society of Cicada 3301 is the first Internet-based secret society known to the public. It officially began with the launch of a puzzle on the Twitter account Cicada 3301 on January 5, 2012. Those who could solve the puzzle used clues from the answer to find a new puzzle. Successive puzzles could be hidden anywhere—on paper signs, in books, social media, and CDs. These puzzles became individualized as the game progressed. Those who solved the entire series of puzzles were granted admission into the society, according to speculation. Cicada 3301 said only that it was seeking highly intelligent individuals. Rumors have spread that it is working on cryptocurrency, a kind of world currency that would be cryptographically protected from hyperinflation, but these claims were unsubstantiated. Cicada 3301 launched a new "beginning" puzzle on Twitter every January 5 until 2014. It is no longer seeking recruits (at least not through Twitter) as of January 2015.

THE (NOT SO) SECRET SERVICE

THE ALTRUISM OF THE SHRINERS

The Ancient Arabic Order of the Nobles of the Mystic Shrine (also known as the Shriners) is a form of Freemasonry known for its altruism. Established in 1870 for the sole purpose of having fun, it turned into an international philanthropic organization with lodges in North America, South America, Europe, and Australia. Freemasons Walter Fleming, a physician, and William J. Florence, an actor, pioneered the order. Fleming and Florence had sat in on a casual discussion among fellow Masons about a new order focused on fun and

In 1994, *The Chronicle of Philanthropy* ranked Shriners Hospitals as the ninth most popular charity or nonprofit in America out of the 100 organizations listed.

brotherhood. Shortly thereafter, Florence went on tour in France and North Africa, where he attended a series of musical comedies about secret societies. Florence was inspired by the comedies, and when he came home he formed fun-oriented Masonry based on those musicals. Fleming liked his ideas and reshaped them to become the rituals and costumes of the Ancient Arabic Order. The order was initiated in New York City on August 13, 1870. Within 12 months the group had initiated another 11 men.

The Shriners' popularity grew fast. By 1938 there were more than 300,000 members in the United States. Later that year, *Life* magazine journalists were allowed a look inside the Shriners' Mecca Temple in New York City and called it the "No. 1 in prestige, wealth, and show." They are known today for fun parades and processions in mini cars. To become a Shriner, one must already be a master Mason at another lodge. There are also Shriner organizations for women, including Daughters of the Nile (established in 1913) and The Ladies' Oriental Shrine (established in 1903). Members must be over the age of 18 and be related by blood, adoption, or marriage to a master Mason or Shriner.

ARABIC NOBLES

Fleming and Florence named their order the Ancient Arabic Order of the Nobles of the Mystic Shrine to reflect the Middle Eastern garb and rituals they had adopted.

Shriners Hospitals for Children is one of the most well-known philanthropic accomplishments of the Shriners. Comprising 22 hospitals, the network spans the United States, Canada, and Mexico and has been serving children free of cost since 1922. In 1920 an Imperial Council Session of the Shriners voted for the establishment of a Shiners Hospital for Crippled Children, and soon the first hospital was opened in Shreveport, Louisiana. By the early 1930s there were more than 13 children's hospitals in operation. These hospitals continue to deal primarily with orthopedic issues, spinal cord rehabilitation, burn treatment, and cleft lip. Until 2012, any child, regardless of race, nationality, or religion, who was in need of treatment was provided with

free care. By then, however, the Shriners had lost $5 billion in endowments because of plummeting stock market investments. For the first time, the Shriners started billing parents' insurance companies after treatment if the family was insured, but is still providing free care to those without insurance.

Philanthropy has been part of the Shriners' creed since 1889, when they aided the city of Johnstown, Pennsylvania, in the aftermath of the South Fork Dam disaster. By that time, 71 of the 79 temples were focused on volunteerism and charitable donation. With the growth of the fraternity came a stronger emphasis on philanthropy. In 1906, the Shriners gave $25,000 to aid those who had lost homes in the San Francisco earthquake. The idea to hold an imperial court to discuss children's hospitals came on the heels of this spirit of generosity. Years earlier, Shriner Freeland Kendrick was inspired by a visit to the Hospital for Crippled Children in Atlanta. The hospital had been a philanthropic effort of the Scottish Rite and was geared toward meeting the growing need of orthopedic disorders in children. Kendrick spent 1919 and most of 1920 visiting Shriners temples around the world to campaign for a children's hospital of its own. He logged more than 150,000 miles, contributing to the landslide decision at the imperial court to fund hospitals.

A PARTING THOUGHT

"I refuse to join any club
that would have me as a member."

—GROUCHO MARX

BIBLIOGRAPHY

"6c. The Pax Romana." Ancient Civilizations. Accessed April 8, 2015. www. ushistory.org/civ/6c.asp.

"About the AOH." Ancient Order of Hibernians. Accessed April 8, 2015. www.aoh.com/about-the-aoh/.

Admin. "The World's 5 Most Bizarre Secret Societies." Wacky Owl. February 16, 2015. Accessed April 8, 2015. www.wackyowl.com /worlds-5-bizarre-secret-societies/.

"Alapine Herstory." Alapine Community Association Inc. Accessed April 8, 2015. www.alapine.org/herstory.html.

Bell, Chris. "The Internet Mystery that Has the World Baffled." *The Telegraph*. November 25, 2013. Accessed April 8, 2015. www.telegraph. co.uk/technology/internet/10468112/The-internet-mystery-that-has -the-world-baffled.html.

"Black Hand." Spartacus Educational. Accessed April 8, 2015. http://spartacus-educational.com/FWWblackhand.htm.

"Brother of New Life." My Little Illumination. 2014. Accessed April 8, 2015.

Bunson, Matthew. *Encyclopedia of the Roman Empire*. New York, NY: Infobase Publishing, 2009.

Canady, Glenn. "Illuminati Sex Trafficking Secrets That Killed Over 12 People." Before It's News. November 22, 2014. Accessed April 9, 2015. http://beforeitsnews.com/alternative/2014/11/illuminati-sex -trafficking-secrets-that-killed-over-12-people-3066092.html.

"Chronicle of the Emperors." Roman-Empire. Accessed April 8, 2015. www.roman-empire.net/.

———. "Major Battles in Roman History." Accessed April 8, 2015. www.roman-empire.net/diverse/battles.html.

Daily Mail Reporter. "Police Break Up 'Drug-Fueled Orgy' At Masonic Lodge After Finding Women Dancing Naked on Stage and Men Filming Sex Acts." *Daily Mail*. September 1, 2013. Accessed April 8, 2015. www.dailymail.co.uk/news/article-2408655/Police-break-drug-fueled -orgy-Masonic-Lodge-finding-women-dancing-naked-stage-men -filming-sex-acts.html.

Dowbenko, Uri. "Masonic Murders AKA Jack the Ripper." Illuminati Conspiracy Archive. Accessed April 9, 2015. www.conspiracyarchive. com/NWO/Masonic_Ritual_Murders.htm.

"Enforcement Acts." American-Historama. March 2015. Accessed April 9, 2015. www.american-historama.org/1866-1881-reconstruction -era/enforcement-acts.htm.

Erowid. "Hashish/Assassin Myth." Erowid. Accessed April 9, 2015.
www.erowid.org/plants/cannabis/cannabis_info4.shtml.

"Facts, Firsts and Precedents." Fifty-Seventh Presidential Inauguration.
Accessed April 8, 2015. www.inaugural.senate.gov/about/facts-and-firsts.

Flock, Elizabeth. "Bohemian Grove: Where the Rich and Powerful Go to
Misbehave." *The Washington Post*. June 15, 2011. Accessed April 8, 2015.

"Frequently Asked Questions." AskAMason. Accessed April 9, 2015.
http://askafreemason.org/topten/index.htm.

Garrison, Laura Turner. "6 Modern Societies Where Women Literally
Rule." Mental Floss. September 29, 2014. Accessed April 8, 2015.
http://mentalfloss.com/article/31274/6-modern-socieies-where
-women-literally-rule.

Healy, Patrick. "A Ritual Gone Fatally Wrong Puts Light on Masonic
Secrecy." *The New York Times*. March 10, 2004. Accessed April 9, 2015.
www.nytimes.com/2004/03/10/nyregion/a-ritual-gone-fatally-wrong
-puts-light-on-masonic-secrecy.html.

"Jaques de Molay." Wikipedia, last modified March 5, 2015, http://en.
wikipedia.org/wiki/Jacques_de_Molay#Arrest_and_charges.

Kashyap, Karthik. "5 World's Weirded Secret Societies." HubPages.
Accessed April 8, 2015. http://karthikkash.hubpages.com
/hub/5-Worlds-Weirdest-Secret-Societies.

Katz, Jesse. "Welcome to the Hotel California." *Los Angeles Magazine*.
March 2004.

Ku Klux Klan- A Secret History. Documentary. YouTube.
www.youtube.com/watch?v=cayCYpxtIyo.

Lendman, Stephen. "'A True Story of the Bilderberg Group' and What they
May Be Planning Now." Global Research. June 1, 2009. Accessed
April 8, 2015. www.globalresearch.ca/the-true-story-of-the
-bilderberg-group-and-what-they-may-be-planning-now/13808.

Levine, Joshua. "France: Where Freemasons Are Still Feared." Bloomberg
Business. April 19, 2012. Accessed April 9, 2015. www.bloomberg.com
/bw/articles/2012-04-19/france-where-freemasons-are-still-feared.

Marc V. "10 Strange and Obscure Secret Societies." Listverse. March 16,
2014. Accessed April 9, 2015. http://listverse.com/2014/03/16
/10-strange-obscue-secret-societies/.

"Madame Xaintrailles." MasonicDictionary. Accessed April 8, 2015.
www.masonicdictionary.com/xaintrailles.html.

———. "The Bavarian Illuminati." MasonicDictionary. Accessed April 8, 2015. www.masonicdictionary.com/illuminati.html.

Millegan, Kris. "Yale's Skull and Bones Secret Society." Shepard College. Accessed April 8, 2015. www.bibliotecapleyades.net/sociopolitica /esp_sociopol_skullbones04.htm.

O'Meara, James J. "God I'm With a Heathen: The Rebirth of the Manner-bund in Brian de Palma's The Untouchables." Counter-Current Publishing. Accessed April 8, 2015. www.counter-currents.com/2012/04 /brian-de-palmas-the-untouchables/.

"OddFellows," Wikipedia. Last modified April 3, 2015. http://en.wikipedia. org/wiki/Oddfellows.

"Ordo Orientis Templi." St Ichtingargus. Accessed April 8, 2015. www.stichtingargus.nl/vrijmetselarij/r/oto_en.html.

Pennacchia, Robyn. "Miley Cyrus Joined the Illuminati, is Having Sex With Demons." DeathAndTaxes. October 31, 2013. Accessed April 9, 2015 www.deathandtaxesmag.com/208850/miley-cyrus-joined -the-illuminati-is-having-sex-with-demons-says-citizen-journalist -rick-wiles/.

"P.E.O. Sisterhood," Wikipedia. Last modified March 20, 2015. http://en.wikipedia.org/wiki/P.E.O._Sisterhood.

Scaruffi, Piero. "A Timeline of the Roman Empire." Scaruffi. 1999. Accessed April 8, 2015. www.scaruffi.com/politics/romans.html.

Secret Societies Conspiracy Theories History Documentary. Documentary. History Channel. www.youtube.com/watch?v=1KuEOwqpyEE.

Secret Societies Shocking Documentary.Documentary. YouTube. www.youtube.com/watch?v=Fofy1LEFOxk.

"Shriners," Wikipedia. Last modified March 24, 2015. http://en.wikipedia. org/wiki/Shriners.

"Shriners Hospitals for Children," Wikipedia. Last modified April 7 2015. http://en.wikipedia.org/wiki/Shriners_Hospitals_for_Children.

Sora, Steven. *Secret Societies of America's Elite*. Rochester, VT: Inner Traditions Bear Company, 2003.

Spradlin, Michael P. "Friday The 13th and The Knights Templar." Michael P. Spradlin. Accessed April 8, 2015. http://michaelspradlin.com /blog/2013/09/friday-the-13th-and-the-knights-templar/.

Starship Earth. "The Truth Behind Angelina Jolie's 'Preventative Medicine'." Starship Earth: The Bigger Picture. May 17, 2013. Accessed

April 8, 2015. http://starshipearththebigpicture.com/2013/05/17
/the-truth-behind-angelina-jolies-preventive-surgery/.

Swanson, Abigail. "Prince Hall Masons (1784–)." BlackPast. Accessed
April 8, 2015. www.blackpast.org/aaw/prince-hall-masons-1784.

"The Eye in the Pyramid." Grand Lodge of Scotland. Accessed April 8,
2015. www.grandlodgescotland.com/masonic-subjects/masonic
-articles/412-the-eye-in-the-pyramid.

"Thule Society." CrystalLinks. Accessed April 8, 2015. www.
crystalinks.com/thule.html.

Usher, David R. "Feminism: Today's Women's Ku Klux Klan." WND
Commentary. October 31, 2014. Accessed April 8, 2015.

Wasserman, James. "Secret Societies: The Templars and the Assassins:
A Lecture Given at the Masonic Reading Room." JamesWasserman-
Books. November 8, 2006. Accessed April 8, 2015. www.stichtingargus.
nl/vrijmetselarij/r/oto_en.html.

"What is HAARP?" ConspiracyWiki. Accessed April 8, 2015.
http://conspiracywiki.com/articles/haarp/what-is-haarp/.

Zennie, Michael. "New Age Followers Still Waiting for Aliens to Beam
them Up 15 Years After Heaven's Gate Cult Suicides Left 39 People
Dead." Daily Mail. March 26, 2012. Accessed April 8, 2015.

INDEX

CONTINUE THE
CONVERSATION

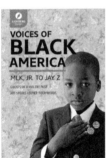

CPSIA information can be obtained at www.ICGtesting.com
Printed in the USA
BVOW07s0203110615

403765BV00002B/3/P